DOLPHIN

By Robert A. Morris
Pictures by Mamoru Funai

A Science I CAN READ Book

SCHOLASTIC BOOK SERVICES
NEW YORK • TORONTO • LONDON • AUCKLAND • SYDNEY • TOKYO

To my wife, Sally

ISBN 0-590-30026-1

12 11 10 9 8 7 6 5   1 2 3 4/8

It is morning.
The large sun comes up
in the sky.
The sea is calm.

TWEET! TWEET! TWEET!
These sounds
are made by dolphins.
They are excited.
They swim around
a large female dolphin.
She is going to have
a baby dolphin.

First, a small tail
comes out of her body.
Then suddenly
her baby is born.
It is three feet long.

The mother dolphin is
eight feet long.

Baby dolphins
are called calves.

Grown-up female dolphins
are called cows.

Grown-up male dolphins
are called bulls.

The new baby is a male.

Dolphins are mammals.
They must breathe air.

The new baby must breathe air soon,
or he will drown.

The mother dolphin
quickly swims under her baby.
She gently pushes him
up to the top of the water.
SWISH! SWISH!

The calf takes his first breath of air.
His nose is on top of his head.
It is called a blowhole.

Now the baby swims by himself.
He will breathe air
when he needs it.

The calf is hungry.
He swims close to his mother.
She turns on her side.
He gets warm milk
from her.

WHIRR. WHIRR. WHIRR.
The dolphins hear a new sound.
It is a ship.
The dolphins swim toward it.
The baby dolphin swims
next to his mother.

The baby dolphin is a fast swimmer.
He moves his tail flukes
up and down.
The flukes push him
through the water.

The fin on top of his back
keeps him from rolling over.

His front fins
are called flippers.
The baby dolphin uses them
to swim up and down
and to turn right or left.

The mother and baby
swim faster and faster.
They race to the front
of the ship.
Then they stop swimming.
They ride on the waves
made by the ship.

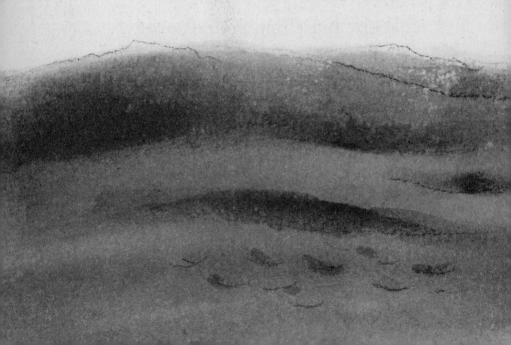

Other dolphins join them.
They dive and jump
and play in the waves.
Their skin is smooth and bare.
It is easy for them
to swim through the water.

It is getting dark.
The dolphins swim away
from the ship.
It is time to rest.
The baby calls to his mother.
TWEET! TWEET! TWEET!
He is hungry
for his mother's milk.

The dolphins rest and breathe
on top of the water.
They will rest
for several hours.
The baby dolphin
closes his eyes.
It has been a long day.

The next morning
the mother dolphin is hungry.
She must find food.

Dolphins hunt together
in a group.
A group of dolphins
is called a pod.

The pods hunt for food
every day.
They eat fish, shrimp,
and small squid.

Today they find
a large school of mackerel.

The mackerel swim away.
But the dolphins are faster.
Some of them swim
below the school of fish.

Some swim to the right,
and some to the left.
Now the mackerel
are all close together.
It is easy
for the dolphins
to catch them.

A wounded fish swims
near the baby dolphin.
The baby quickly grabs it.
But the fish is too large.
The baby cannot hold it in his mouth.
The fish gets away.

CHURP! CHURP! CHURP!
This is the sound
of killer whales.
Killer whales are enemies
of dolphins.
They eat seals, large fish,
and dolphins.

SLAP! SLAP! SLAP!
A dolphin hits the water
with his tail.
That is the signal for danger.
The mother dolphin goes quickly
to her baby.

All the dolphins swim away.
They swim faster and faster.
But the killer whales
are coming closer
and closer.

The baby dolphin is tired.
Some of the bull dolphins
stay near
to protect him.

Then the killer whales
see the large school of mackerel.
They chase the mackerel instead.
The dolphins swim away.
They are safe.

Each day the calf
grows larger and larger.
He is now six months old.
He is over four feet long.
When he is two years old,
he will be
as big as his mother.

Sometimes the mother dolphin
leaves her calf
to dive for food.

While she is gone,
two other cows
watch the baby.
They help the mother dolphin
care for her calf.

The baby dolphin
cannot dive as deep
as his mother.
He can stay under water
for only three minutes.

The mother dolphin can dive
one hundred feet deep.
The deep water is cold.
But she has a thick layer of fat
under her skin.
The fat keeps her warm.
She stays under water
for six minutes.

The mother dolphin comes back
with a fish in her mouth.
She lets the fish go.
She wants the calf
to catch it by himself.

The calf chases the fish
and holds it with his teeth.
His small teeth are not like
baby teeth.
He will keep them
all of his life.
They will grow bigger
as he grows bigger.

The calf does not chew the fish.
He swallows it whole.

WHIRR. WHIRR. WHIRR.
A shrimp boat is coming.

Men pull in the large nets.
The nets are full of
shrimp and fish.
The men take the shrimp,
but they do not want the fish.
They throw them back into the sea.
The dolphins swim up quickly
and eat the fish.

Sometimes the water is muddy.
The dolphins cannot see the fish.

CLICK! CLICK! CLICK!
The dolphins make
special sounds.
These sounds go through the water.
They hit the fish
and bounce back
to the dolphins.

These sounds
tell the dolphins
where the fish are.

CLICK! CLICK! CLICK!
The baby dolphin swims
back and forth
eating small fish.

Suddenly, there is a huge animal
in the muddy water.
It is much bigger than
the mother dolphin.
It is a giant tiger shark.
The shark is after the fish, too.

SLAP! SLAP! SLAP!
One of the dolphins
makes the danger sound.
It is too late!
The shark catches the baby dolphin
by the flipper.

The little dolphin
is wounded.
The tip of his flipper
is gone.

Many bull dolphins
swim toward the shark.
They hit the shark
with their beaks.
The shark is hurt.
He swims away.

The baby dolphin
needs air.
Two dolphins swim
under him.
They push him up
to the top of the water.
Now he can breathe.

The dolphin pod
stays near the baby
to protect him.
He is not hurt badly.
His flipper will soon heal.

TWEET! TWEET! TWEET!
The mother dolphin is calling.
The baby dolphin rushes
to her side.
It is time to get milk.

After he is one-year-old,
the dolphin calf
will not need milk.
He will be able
to care for himself.

The dolphin may live for thirty years.
He will stay with the pod
for a long time.

AUTHOR'S NOTE

This story is about a young bottlenosed dolphin. Its scientific name is *Tursiops truncatus*. Bottlenosed dolphins are found along the Atlantic coasts of the United States and Europe. In captivity they are easily trained and are very friendly toward people.